THE BARE BONES CAMERA COURSE FOR FILM AND VIDEO

(SECOND EDITION, REVISED)

By Tom Schroeppel

Illustrations by Persistence of Vision/Edward Fiol

THE BARE BONES CAMERA COURSE FOR FILM AND VIDEO (SECOND EDITION, REVISED). Copyright (c)1982-2010 by Tom Schroeppel. All rights reserved. Printed in the United States of America. No parts of this book may be used or reproduced in any manner whatsoever without written permission, except in the case of brief quotations embodied in critical articles and reviews. For information, address Tom Schroeppel, 3205 West Price Avenue, Tampa, Florida 33611-3720.

LIBRARY OF CONGRESS CATALOG CARD NUMBER 82-90651

10-Digit ISBN 0-9603718-1-8

13-Digit ISBN 9 780960 371815

36th Printing

Manufactured in the United States of America

TABLE OF CONTENTS

PREFACE

This book explains, as simply as possible, how to shoot usable images on film, tape and other media.

If you are, or plan to be, a cameraperson, I suggest you read your camera's operator's manual in addition to this book. When you understand both, you should be able to go out and shoot footage that works.

If you're not interested in becoming a cameraperson, but simply want to better understand how the camera is used, no additional reading is required. Just relax and enjoy the book.

1. Basics

THE CAMERA - HOW IT WORKS

The camera is an imperfect imitation of the human eye. Like the eye, it sees by means of a lens which gathers light reflected off objects. The lens directs this light onto a surface which senses the pattern formed by the differences in brightness and color of the different parts of the scene. In the case of the eye, this surface at the back of the eye sends the pattern of light to the brain where it is translated into an image which we "see."

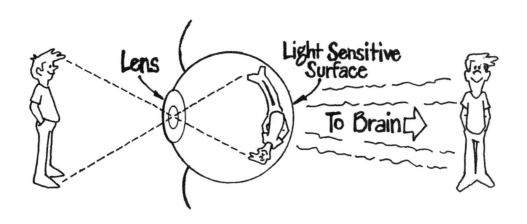

THE EYE GATHERS PATTERNS OF REFLECTED LIGHT WHICH THE BRAIN TRANSLATES INTO IMAGES WE SEE.

In the case of the camera, the lens directs the patterns of light onto a variety of sensitive surfaces. Still film cameras record light patterns on film coated with light-sensitive chemicals. The chemicals react differently to different amounts and colors of light, forming a record, or image, of the light pattern. After the film is processed in other chemicals, the image becomes visible.

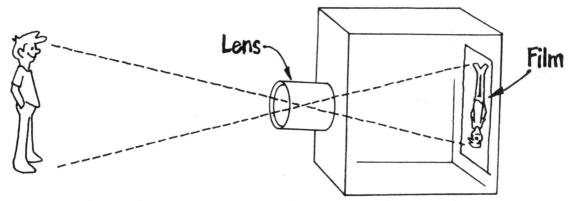

*STILL FILM CAMERAS RECORD LIGHT PATTERNS ON FILM
COATED WITH LIGHT-SENSITIVE CHEMICALS*

You'll notice that both the lens of the eye and the lens of the camera turn the light pattern upside down as it passes through. This is because they're both convex lenses, or lenses which curve outward. Because of their physical properties, convex lenses always invert images. In the brain, and in the camera viewfinder, the images are turned right side up again.

Movie cameras record images in the same way as still film cameras, except they do it more often. Eight-millimeter movie cameras normally take 18 different pictures, or frames, every second. Sixteen millimeter and thirty-five millimeter movie cameras take 24 frames per second. When these pictures are projected on a screen at the same fast rate, they give the illusion of continuous movement. The viewer's mind fills in the gaps between the individual frames, due to a physiological phenomenon known as persistence of vision.

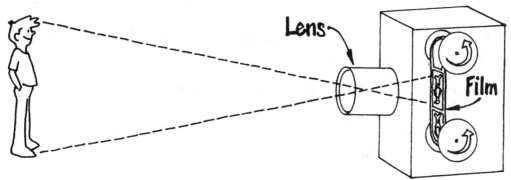

MOVIE CAMERAS TAKE MANY DIFFERENT PICTURES EVERY SECOND.

In digital cameras-both still and video-the lens focuses light patterns onto a light-sensitive surface made up of small flat chips called charge coupled devices, or CCDs. Each CCD contains thousands of tiny light-sensitive areas called picture elements, or pixels, which change according to the color and intensity of the light hitting them. In video cameras, the image formed by all the pixels taken together is electronically collected off the chip at a rate of either 25 or 30 complete images per second. These images can then be recorded or broadcast.

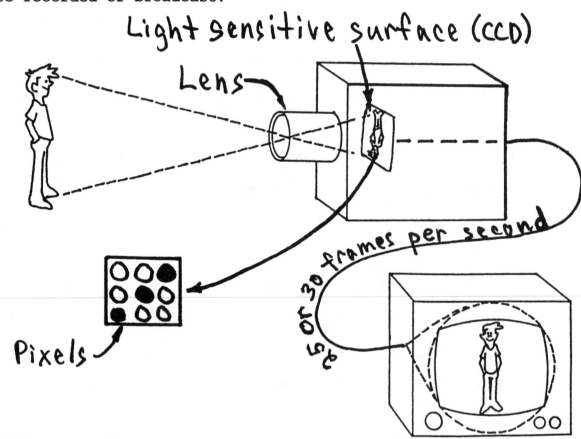

VIDEO CAMERAS CONVERT LIGHT PATTERNS INTO ELECTRONIC IMAGES

At the viewfinder or TV set the process is reversed to recreate the original image. Persistence of vision causes the viewer to perceive the separate pictures, or frames, as continuous movement.

EXPOSURE

Exposure is the amount of light that comes through the lens and hits the film or CCD chip. The hole in the center of the lens that the light travels through is called the aperture. If the aperture is big, it lets in lots of light. If it's small, it lets in very little light. The size of the aperture is adjusted by the f/stop ring on the outside of the lens. An f/stop is simply a measure of how big or how little the aperture is.

I find that the easiest way to understand f/stops is to think of them in terms of fractions, because that's what they really are. F/2 means that the aperture is 1/2 as big across as the lens is long. F/16 means that the aperture is 1/16th as big across as the lens is long.

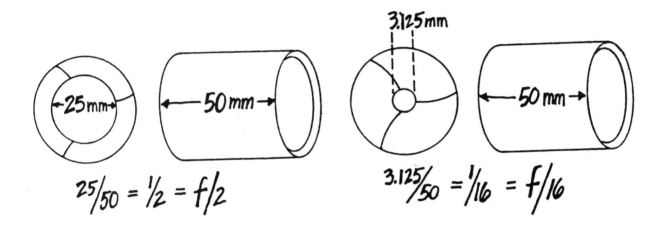

When you look at it this way, it's easy to understand why in a dark room, you'll probably be shooting at f/2 to let in all the light you can. Conversely, outside in bright sunlight, where you've got a lot of light, you'll probably stop down to f/11 or f/16, to let less light in.

Now that you understand that, let me point out that in most
modern lenses, especially zoom lenses, what I've just told you isn't
absolutely true. An f/2 aperture won't physically be exactly 1/2 the
length of the lens. But optically it will be. It will let through
as much light as if it were indeed 1/2 the length of the lens. And
that's the important thing.

F/stops are constructed so that as you go from f/1 to f/22 and
beyond, each stop admits 1/2 as much light as the one before. The
progression is: f/1, f/1.4, f/2, f/2.8, f/4, f/5.6, f/8, f/11, f/16,
f/22, f/32, f/45, f/64, and so on. F/1.4 admits half as much light
as f/1. F/4 admits half as much light as f/2.8.

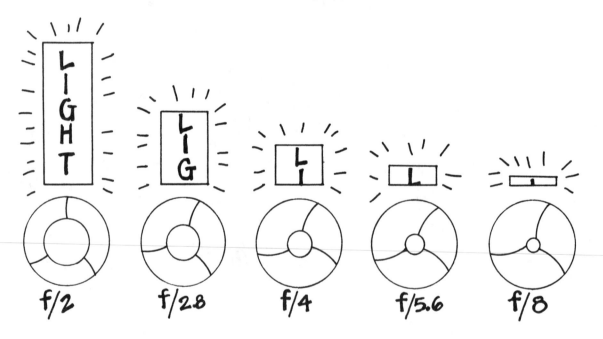

EACH F/STOP ADMITS HALF AS MUCH LIGHT AS THE ONE BEFORE.

Many of the newer lenses are marked in both f/stops and T/stops,
or T/stops alone. T/stops are more accurately measured f/stops.
F/4 on one lens may not let in exactly the same amount of light as
f/4 on another lens; but T/4 is the same on every lens. It always
lets in the same amount of light.

COLOR TEMPERATURE

Have you ever been out walking on a cold, dingy day and remarked to yourself how warm and cozy all the lighted windows looked? Well, that was because the light in the windows <u>was</u> of a warmer color than the light outside.

Yes, light comes in different colors. If you think about it, you'll see it's true. There's the red glow from an open fire or a sunset; the bluish cast of a sky dark with rainclouds; and that blue-green ghoulish look you get from the fluorescents in all-night pizzerias. As a general rule, our eyes adjust so well to these different colored light sources that we hardly notice them. Not so the camera.

Color films and CCD chips can handle only one color of light source at a time and reproduce colors accurately. They do this by means of <u>color temperature</u> and <u>color filters</u>.

<u>Color temperature</u> is a way to identify different colors of light sources. It's measured in degrees Kelvin, after Lord Kelvin, who devised the system. It's written like this: 2500K.

The idea is, you take a perfectly black body, like a piece of coal, at absolute zero (-273°C), and start heating it up. As it gets hotter, it puts out different colors of light: first red, then blue, then bluish-white. The different colors of light are identified by the temperatures at which they occur. 2000K is the reddish light produced at 2000 degrees Kelvin. 8000K is the bluish light produced at 8000 degrees Kelvin.

As I mentioned above, color films and CCDs can handle only one color of light source at a time. To take pictures under a different colored light source, <u>color filters</u> are used to convert the existing light to the color temperature required.

Professional video cameras have built-in filters, which you set according to the light you'll be shooting under. A typical filter selection might include: TUNGSTEN-INCANDESCENT (3200K); MIXED TUNGSTEN AND DAYLIGHT/FLUORESCENT (4300K); DAYLIGHT (5400K); AND SHADE (6600K). (Fluorescent light, strictly speaking, has a discontinuous spectrum and doesn't fit into the Kelvin system; still, a 4300K filter setting will give you adequate color reproduction.)

Once you select the correct filter on a video camera, fine tune the color by adjusting your white balance. This procedure varies from camera to camera and can be as simple as pushing a single button. It assures that the whites in your scene reproduce as whites; the other colors then fall into place.

Color movie films are manufactured for two kinds of light: 3200K-Tungsten; and 5400K-Daylight. If you shoot tungsten film in tungsten light, you don't need a filter. Likewise if you shoot daylight film in daylight.

To shoot tungsten film in daylight, put a #85 filter on the front of the lens or in a filter slot on the camera. This orange filter converts 5400K bluish daylight to reddish 3200K tungsten.

To shoot daylight film inside with tungsten light, use a #80A filter. This blue filter converts reddish tungsten light to bluish daylight. For photoflood lights (3400K) use a #80B filter.

SETTING EXPOSURE ON A VIDEO CAMERA

First, select the correct filter and adjust your white balance, as discussed above.

If your camera has automatic exposure and you can't turn it off, all you can do is avoid large light areas and large dark areas within the frame. These will throw your exposure off.

Professional video cameras have both auto and manual exposure. To manually change your exposure, look in the viewfinder and move the f/stop ring until the picture looks good. (Most cameras also have an indicator in the viewfinder to tell you when your exposure is correct.) With a new or strange camera, it's a good idea to make a test recording under various lighting conditions and play it back on a good monitor to check the calibration of your camera's viewfinder. Sometimes you'll have to go a little darker or a little lighter in the viewfinder to get the best color on playback.

The main problem with video cameras is large areas of white, particularly those caused by strong backlight-light shining toward the camera from behind the subject. If you include too much pure, bright white in your frame, all the other colors go dark. Sometimes the white will "bleed" over into the other colors. White problems are seen clearly in your viewfinder, so they're easily avoidable by moving the camera or subject or both, or by changing your lighting or scenery.

SETTING EXPOSURE ON A FILM CAMERA

ISO. Check the film label to see what ISO your film is. ISO stands for International Standards Organization. The ISO number indicates the speed or sensitivity of the film. The lower the number, the less sensitive, the "slower" the film is, and the more light you need to get a usable picture. The higher the number, the more sensitive, the "faster" the film is, and the less light you need to get a usable picture.

Film speed may also be indicated as ASA, for American Standards Association, or EI, for Exposure Index. For all practical purposes, ASA and EI numbers are equivalent to ISO numbers.

ISO numbers progress geometrically in terms of sensitivity. Each time you double the ISO number, you halve the amount of light needed to get a usable image.

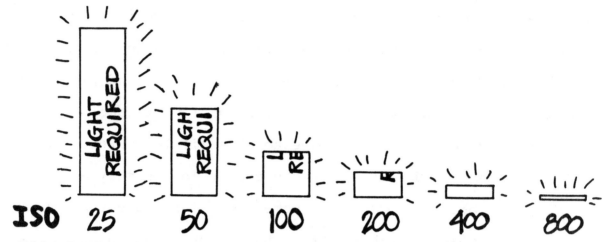

EACH TIME YOU DOUBLE THE ISO, YOU CUT YOUR LIGHT REQUIREMENT IN HALF.

Slower, low ISO films generally produce a higher quality picture. Faster, higher ISO films, while requiring much less light, generally produce grainier, lower quality images.

COLOR TEMPERATURE. Make sure the color temperature of your film is the same as the color temperature of the light you're filming under. If not, put on a #85 filter to use tungsten film in daylight; or put on a #80A filter to use daylight film in tungsten light.

Remember, any time you use a filter on the camera, you're reducing the amount of light reaching the film. This means you have to have that much more light entering the lens, to compensate for the light soaked up by the filter. Since your light requirements have gone up, you've effectively lowered your ISO. Look once more at the chart above and you'll see what I mean: higher light requirement equals lower ISO number. To determine the correct ISO for the film-filter combination you're using, check the manufacturer's information sheet for that particular film.

LIGHT METERS.   Light meters measure the amount of light hitting them.   Then, based on the ISO of your film and the number of frames per second you're shooting, they tell you what f/stop to set for the best exposure of your scene.

For all intents and purposes, light meters see everything in black and white, in terms of lightness and darkness.   They don't react to the color of a subject, only to its lightness or darkness.

On most cameras with built-in meters and on hand-held light meters you must manually set the ISO.   The method varies, but be sure you do it.   Otherwise, the meter won't know how much light your film requires and will give you incorrect exposures.

Overexposure means you let too much light in--the picture is too light, washed out.   *Underexposure* means you didn't let enough light in--the picture is too dark.

USING A LIGHT METER.   If you have an automatic exposure camera and you can't manually override it, all you can do is try to avoid large light and dark areas in your frame, which will throw your exposure off.

On-camera exposure meters are called *reflective* meters.   They measure the light *reflected* at the camera by whatever it is you're pointing the camera at.   Handheld reflective meters work the same way.

ON-CAMERA AND HANDHELD REFLECTIVE LIGHT METERS MEASURE LIGHT REFLECTED OFF THE SUBJECT.

Reflective meters work on the basis of a theoretical average subject which is gray and reflects 18% of the light hitting it.   (You can buy an 18% Gray Card from Kodak.)   No matter where you point it, the meter will tell you the f/stop needed to reproduce that subject as if it were 18% gray. This usually gives you a satisfactory exposure. However, for lighter-than-average gray subjects, you have to open up your aperture to reproduce the subject as lighter than 18% gray. For darker-than-average subjects, close down to let less light in and re-produce the subject correctly as darker than 18% gray. How much, you have to learn by experience.

For most film work, the best way to measure light is with a hand-held *incident* light meter. The incident meter has a white half-sphere which you hold in front of your subject, pointing toward the camera. The meter measures the light falling on that particular spot and cal-culates an f/stop for an average 18% gray subject. (It's essentially the same as taking a reflective reading off a gray card held in front of your subject.) This gives you the correct exposure for almost any subject, since once you set your exposure correctly for 18% gray, all the other reflectance values fall into place. A white subject with 90% reflectance reproduces as 90% white. 0% black reproduces as 0% black. 50% gray reproduces as 50% gray. And so on.

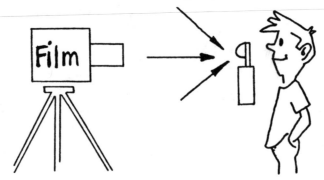

INCIDENT LIGHT METERS MEASURE LIGHT FALLING ON THE SUBJECT.

Normally, the only time you have to adjust an incident reading is when you *want* to reproduce something darker or lighter than it really is. For example, you might want to open up your aperture to lighten and show more detail in a very black face; or close down and darken a very white face to see more detail in it.

LENSES

The human eye is a wonder. With a single lens, it can concentrate on a tiny detail of a scene, excluding all else, and in the next instant take in a whole panorama. Unfortunately, the camera is not so versatile. It requires many different lenses to even approximate the performance of the eye.

Every camera has one lens which is considered the "normal" lens. This is the lens which comes closest to reproducing objects with the same perspective as the human eye; that is, objects appear to be the same size, proportion and distance as if we weren't looking through the camera at all, but seeing them with the naked eye. The normal lens usually includes a horizontal area of about 25 degrees.

On a sixteen millimeter camera, the normal lens has a focal length (its optical measurement) of 25 millimeters. On a 35-millimeter camera, it's 50 millimeters long. On a video camera with a 2/3" CCD chip, the normal lens is 25 millimeters long.

The other lenses on the camera are classified "wide angle" if they include a larger area that the normal lens, and "telephoto" if they include a smaller area.

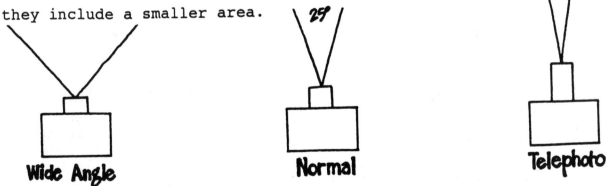

Wide Angle   Normal   Telephoto

Wide angle lenses are shorter than normal lenses; telephoto lenses are longer. If your normal lens is 25mm, your wide angle might be 12mm and your telephoto 100mm.

Wide angle and telephoto lenses have special characteristics which can be summarized as follows:

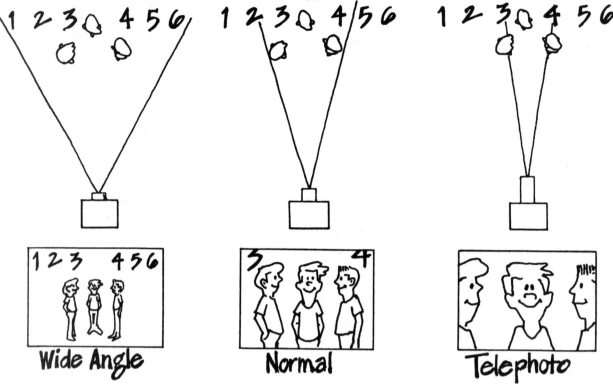

Wide Angle

Normal

Telephoto

* Includes a larger area than the normal lens at the same distance--good for cramped quarters where you can't move the camera back any farther.

* Subject is smaller in the frame than with the normal lens at the same distance.

* Exaggerates depth-- makes elements appear farther apart than normal.

* Because of exaggerated distances, movements toward and away from the camera seem faster than normal. Move 6 inches toward the camera and it looks like you're moving 18 inches.

* Because of smaller image size, camera jiggles are less noticeable. Good for handholding the camera.

* Includes a smaller area than the normal lens at the same distance--good for distant subjects where you can't move the camera closer.

* Subject is larger in the frame than with the normal lens at the same distance.

* Compresses depth--makes elements appear closer together than normal.

* Because of compressed distances, movements toward and away from the camera seem slower than normal. Move 18 inches toward the camera and it looks like you're moving 6 inches.

* Because of larger image size, camera jiggles are more noticeable. Bad for handholding the camera.

Wide angle and telephoto lenses reproduce faces in different ways:

Wide Angle

Features become spread out, bulbous.

Normal

Telephoto

Features become flattened out, compressed.

The more extreme wide angle lenses suffer from geometric distortion. Vertical and horizontal lines become curved near the edges of the frame. This is called *pincushioning*.

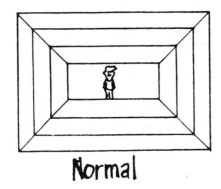

Normal

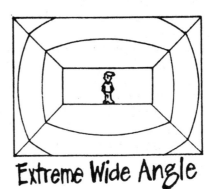

Extreme Wide Angle

FOCUS. The healthy human eye normally sees images in focus--that is, sharp and clear, not blurry. This is because the lens of the eye automatically brings each light ray to a sharp point on the light-sensitive surface at the back of the eye. The pattern formed by all these sharp points of light taken together forms a clear, sharp image.

Automatic focus cameras, which emulate the eye, don't always work the way you want them to. When you have the time, it's usually best to do the focusing yourself.

To focus a camera which doesn't have through-the-lens viewing, you measure or estimate the distance of the subject from the camera, then move the focus ring on the lens to that setting.

Focusing is easier, quicker and surer on cameras with through-the-lens viewing systems. This is because there's no guesswork involved--what you see is what you get. All you do is look in the viewfinder and turn the focus ring on the lens till your subject looks sharp and clear. (If possible on a film camera, you should open the lens to its widest aperture for focusing--I'll explain why in the following section on depth of field.)

Some cameras have focusing eyepieces, which use little diopter rings to adjust the focus of the image in the viewfinder to the individual eye of the cameraperson. Adjustable eyepieces are especially useful for people who wear glasses but who prefer or need to shoot without them. (It's not a good idea to wear glasses when shooting with a through-the-lens film camera--light entering the viewing system from around the edges of your glasses can fog the film.)

If your camera has a focusing eyepiece, do adjust it to your eye--otherwise you'll never see a perfectly sharp image through the lens and you'll never be 100% sure of your focus.

To adjust a focusing eyepiece, first point the camera at a bright area--the sky, or a white wall, for example. Open the lens to its widest aperture. Throw the lens out of focus--turn the focus ring until everything is as blurry as possible. Then, on a film camera, turn the diopter ring on the eyepiece until the ground glass of the viewfinder screen is in focus--until the textured surface of the screen is as sharp and clear as possible. On a video camera, adjust the diopter ring until the messages on the viewfinder screen are as sharp as possible. That's all there is to it. Now you're ready to focus the lens with complete confidence.

ZOOM LENSES. Most cameras use a zoom lens, which combines a wide range of focal lengths in a single lens. By moving a single control, you can switch from wide angle to normal to telephoto, or anywhere in between, without changing lenses. This makes it a lot easier and quicker to compose your shots. If you want a little wider frame, zoom back to wide angle; for a closer shot, zoom in to telephoto.

There's a special way to focus a zoom lens. First, zoom all the way in on your subject, with the lens in maximum telephoto position. Focus the lens, even if all you see is an eyeball. Then zoom out wide and find your final framing. Your subject will remain sharp and in focus at any zoom setting, as long as neither the camera or the subject changes position. (When possible on a film camera, you should also open the lens to its widest aperture for focusing--we'll learn why in the following section on depth of field.)

DEPTH OF FIELD

Depth of field is simply the area in front of your camera where everything looks sharp and in focus. For example, if you're focused on somebody standing 10 feet in front of the camera, your depth of field might be from 8 feet to 14 feet. That means objects falling within that area will be acceptably sharp and in focus; objects falling outside the area will be soft and out of focus.

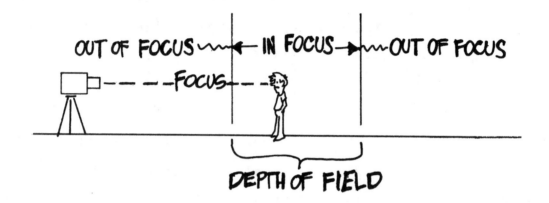

There are several important things to know about depth of field. First is this: *Your depth of field decreases as you increase your focal length.* In other words, with a telephoto lens you have a much shallower area in focus than with a normal lens. That's why with a zoom lens, you zoom in to telephoto for focusing--it makes it easier to see the exact point where your subject is sharpest.

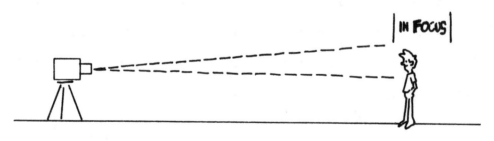

TELEPHOTO = LESS DEPTH OF FIELD

The next thing to know is: *Your depth of field increases as you decrease your focal length.* With a wide angle lens, you have a much deeper area in focus than with a normal lens. This is why, when you're shooting in uncontrolled situations with a zoom lens and don't have time to zoom in and check focus, you're better off setting an approximate focus and staying at wide angle. This will give you your best chance of keeping everything in acceptable focus.

WIDE ANGLE = GREATER DEPTH OF FIELD

Another thing about depth of field: *Your depth of field increases as you close down your aperture.* At f/16 you have more depth of field than at f/2. When you make your aperture smaller, it's essentially the same as squinting your eyes to see something sharper in the distance. This is why on film cameras we open the lens to it's widest aperture to focus: it makes it easier to see the exact focus point.

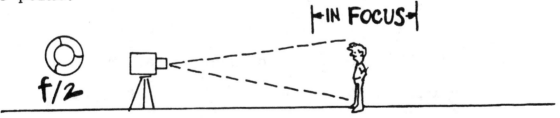

LARGE APERTURE = LESS DEPTH OF FIELD

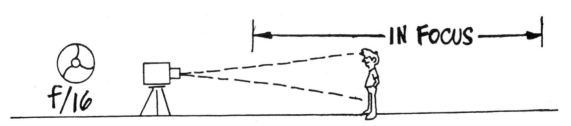

SMALL APERTURE = GREATER DEPTH OF FIELD

Next: *Your depth of field increases as your subject gets
farther from the camera.* The farther away the subject, the more
depth of field; the closer the subject, the less depth of field.

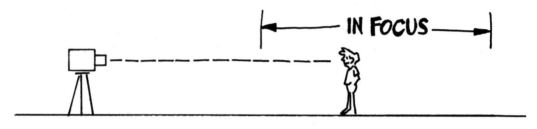

DISTANT SUBJECT = GREATER DEPTH OF FIELD

CLOSE SUBJECT = LESS DEPTH OF FIELD

Finally: *You always have less depth of field in front of your
point of focus than behind it.* This is especially noticeable at
distances of 25 feet or less. At these near distances, you can
usually figure on your depth of field extending approximately 1/3
in front and 2/3 behind your point of focus. So, if you're working
with a shallow depth of field and you want to take maximum advantage
of it, focus on a point 1/3 of the way into the area you want in
focus.

FOCUSING IN THE MIDDLE LEAVES THE FRONT MAN OUT OF FOCUS.

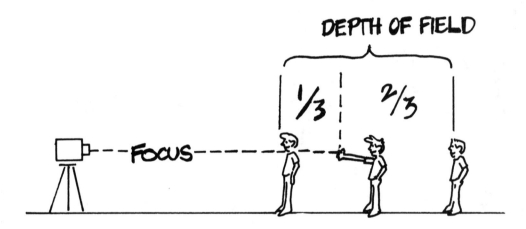

FOCUSING ON A POINT 1/3 OF THE WAY IN PUTS EVERYBODY IN FOCUS.

2. COMPOSITION

THE CAMERA - A TOOL FOR SELECTIVE VISION

The camera is a tool for looking at things in a special way. It's a window on the world which you control. Your viewer--the person who will look at the pictures you take--will see only what you decide to show him. This selectivity is the basis of all camerawork.

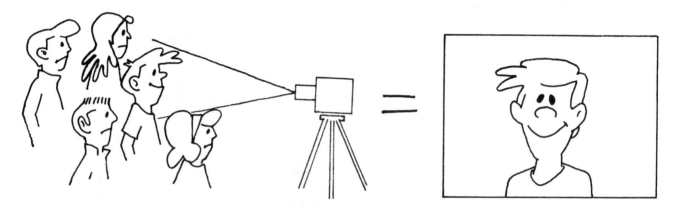

THE CAMERA IS SELECTIVE. YOU DECIDE WHAT THE VIEWER WILL SEE

Say you're shooting a program about a high school. The decisions you as a cameraperson make will shape the reality of the school as perceived by your viewer. Leave Student A out of your frame and for your viewer he will never exist. Include B, C, and D in a number of shots and they become important persons. Show E studying by himself and he becomes a loner. By choosing what to shoot and how to shoot it, you create your own selective version of the high school. How close your version comes to reality depends on your camera skills and how you use them.

USE A TRIPOD

To appreciate a good composition, the viewer must first see it without distractions. One of the most common distractions is camera jiggle caused by shaky handholding of the camera.

Shaky pictures are okay if you're shooting an earthquake, or if you're in the middle of a prison riot or some other precarious situation. Most of the time, though, shaky pictures are just plain annoying to the viewer. They make it harder for him to see what's happening and they remind him of the camera; they destroy the illusion that's he's seeing the real thing.

In editing scenes together, the only thing more distracting than a shaky shot of a building inserted between two nice steady shots is two different shaky shots one after the other, with one shaking up and down and the other shaking side to side. Where they come together, it looks like the cut was made with a chain saw.

So use a tripod whenever possible. A good tripod, preferably with a fluid head, will give you a steady frame, make your camera moves smoother, and keep your arms and the rest of your body from getting tired so quickly.

It's not that much trouble to use a tripod. With practice, most people can set up and level a tripod in less than 30 seconds. But, if you don't have a tripod, or you're someplace where a tripod would get in the way, or you're just moving too fast to bother with it, you can still try for tripod-like support. Use a monopod or a shoulder brace. Lean against a wall, a chair, or your assistant. Try for at least three points of support for the camera. With a well-balanced news camera, these would be your shoulder, your hand on the grip, and the side of your head. If you can brace the elbow of your camera-supporting arm against your side, so much the better.

RULE OF THIRDS

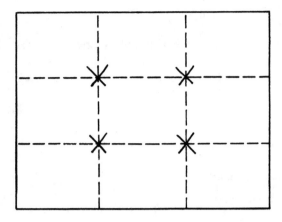

    The rule of thirds is an old, old theory about composition that still works pretty well. It won't compose the picture for you, but it'll at least give you someplace to start.

    The idea is to mentally divide the frame into thirds horizontally and vertically. Then you place your elements along the lines, preferably with the center of interest at one of the four points where the lines cross.

    Here are some examples of compositions improved by using the rule of thirds:

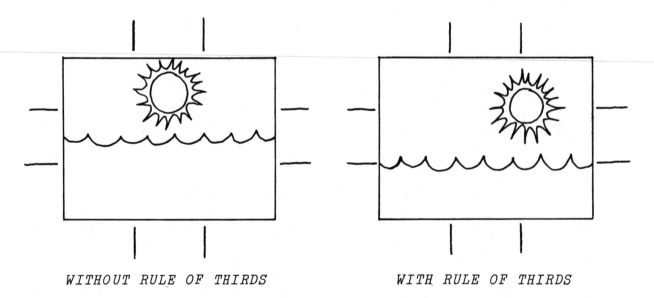

WITHOUT RULE OF THIRDS   *WITH RULE OF THIRDS*

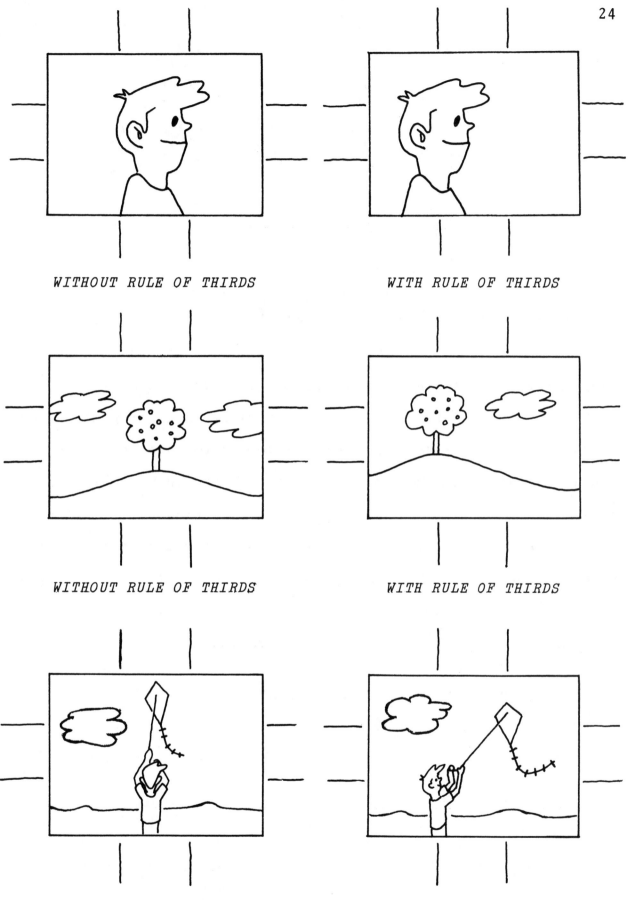

WITHOUT RULE OF THIRDS

WITH RULE OF THIRDS

WITHOUT RULE OF THIRDS

WITH RULE OF THIRDS

WITHOUT RULE OF THIRDS

WITH RULE OF THIRDS

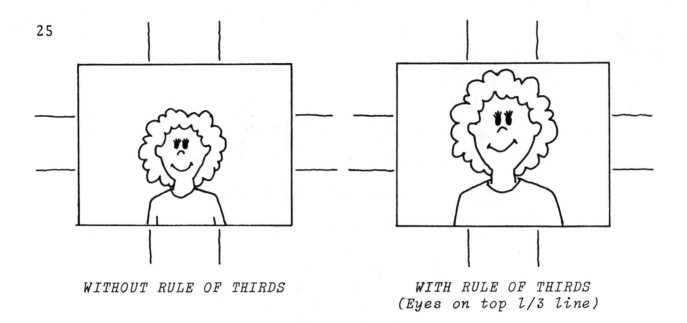

WITHOUT RULE OF THIRDS

WITH RULE OF THIRDS
(Eyes on top 1/3 line)

In paintings, still photos and feature films, you'll see many interesting and good compositions that don't comply with the rule of thirds. But remember, such compositions, being more complicated, require more time from the viewer to comprehend. His eye will roam around more before he sees what you want him to see. If you can afford to leave an unusual composition on the screen 15 or 20 seconds or more, it can work--often quite nicely. But be sure you know what you're doing and why. For most documentary film and TV work, the rule of thirds is a good safe bet.

BALANCE - LEADING LOOKS

One of the most common errors among camerapersons everywhere
is the failure to leave enough space in front of people's faces
when they're looking to one side or the other.

A shot like this,

is annoying to look at. Psychologically, the viewer perceives the
man as boxed in, with no place to go. By moving the frame just a
little, like this,

you get a more comfortable composition. You've allowed for the
compositional weight of the look.

People aren't the only things that have looks. Almost everything has a look. Some examples follow on the next page.

LEADING LOOKS - CONTINUED

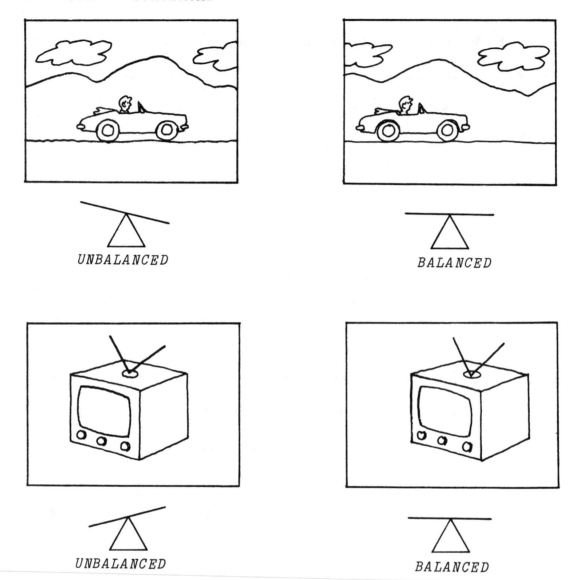

UNBALANCED   BALANCED

UNBALANCED   BALANCED

UNBALANCED   BALANCED

BALANCE - MASSES

Sometimes you see a scene with a large object on one side and nothing significant on the other side. Even though it doesn't look all that bad, you still feel a little uneasy about it. That's because it's off balance in terms of mass. This is most pleasantly corrected by placing a smaller object at some distance away within the frame. Visual leverage then balances the two nicely, like this:

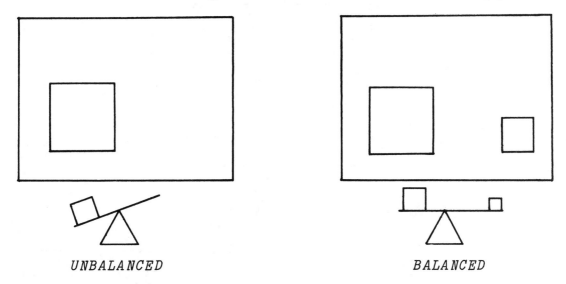

UNBALANCED   BALANCED

Of course you can balance out with another object the same size in the frame, but it usually ends up kind of static and un-exciting:

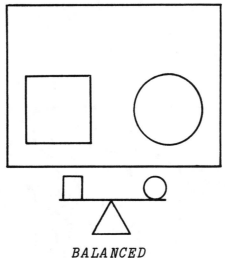

BALANCED

Remember, when we're balancing masses we're not concerned
with the true size of things. All that matters is how big they
look through the camera. Objects closer to the camera will always
appear larger; those farther away will appear smaller. Depending
on the camera angle, a house in the distance can balance out a
man in the foreground:

Some other examples:

BALANCE - COLORS

The most important thing to know about colors is that bright ones attract the viewer's eye. How often have you seen a TV interview on location somewhere and found yourself watching, not the interview, but some guy in a red shirt in the background? Your eye just naturally goes to white or brightly colored areas in the frame. Once you know this fact, you can use it to help your pictures.

First off, try to arrange your frame so that the brightest area is also the area you want the viewer to look at first. Consider the following example, where we want the viewer to look at the man:

NO GOOD

EYE GOES TO THE WALL INSTEAD OF THE MAN

BETTER

EYE GOES TO THE MAN

When you do include a bright object or area in your frame, remember that its brightness gives it extra weight in the composition-- weight you have to balance out, either with another bright area, or with a larger mass.

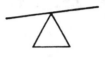

OFF-BALANCE

Although the masses of the flower and the pot balance out, the brightness of the flower pulls the composition to the left.

BALANCED

The brightness of the pot now balances out the brightness of the flower.

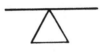

BALANCED

Here the brightness of the flower is balanced out by placing a
larger mass on the other side of the frame.

ANGLES

Reality has three physical dimensions: height, width, and depth. In pictures we have only two dimensions: height and width. To give the illusion of depth, we show things at an angle, so we can at least see two sides.

FLAT   ANGLED

FLAT   ANGLED

The angle created by the difference in height between the camera and the subject makes a definite impression on the viewer:

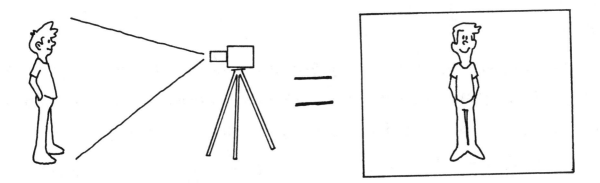

When the camera and the subject are at the same height, it gives the feeling that the viewer and the subject are of equal value.

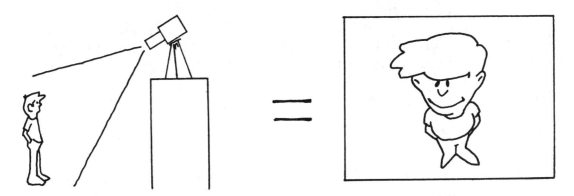

When the camera is higher than the subject, it gives the feeling that the subject is inferior, smaller, less important.

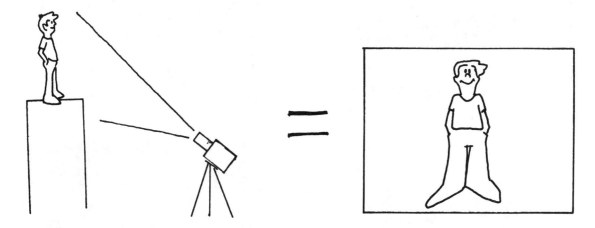

When the camera is lower than the subject, it gives the feeling that the subject is superior, larger, more important.

By raising or lowering your camera, you can subtly influence how your viewer will perceive your subject. This is used to great effect in horror films and political TV commercials.

FRAMES WITHIN THE FRAME

Often you can make a picture more interesting by using elements
of your location to create full or partial frames within the camera
frame.

OKAY

BETTER

OKAY

BETTER

OKAY

BETTER

This type of framing can also be used to hide or obstruct unwanted elements. For example, a cut tree branch held near the camera can cover up an ugly sky or a billboard in the background.

NO GOOD

BETTER

LEADING LINES

A nice way to direct the viewer's eye to your subject is through the use of leading lines. Here are some examples:

Viewer's eye is drawn here

NOT VERY GOOD

BETTER

Lines of fence now lead to man.

Viewer's eye is drawn here

NOT VERY GOOD

From this angle, the path leads away from the house.

BETTER

From this angle, the path leads toward the house.

Viewer's eye is drawn here

NOT VERY GOOD

The lines lead away from
the flower on the table.

BETTER

All lines now lead to the
flower on the table

BACKGROUNDS

The best background is the one that stays where it belongs--
in the background. Unfortunately, some types of backgrounds push
forward and call attention away from your foreground subjects.
Let's look at some of the more common distracting backgrounds and
ways to avoid them:

PROBLEM: Door frames, window frames, trees, poles, etc., that
grow out of people's heads.

SOLUTION: Move the camera, the subject, or both.

PROBLEM: Backgrounds that are too visually busy, so full of details and colors similar to those of the subject that the subject becomes buried in the background.

SOLUTION #1: Move the camera, the subject, or both.

SOLUTION #2: Move the camera far enough back from the subject

so you can use a telephoto focal length. This will give you a
more shallow depth of field, throwing the background out of focus
while leaving the subject sharp.

PROBLEM: Unusual or persistent movements in the background.
SOLUTION: Move the camera, the subject, or both.

One quick way to remove a distracting background element from
your frame is to move closer to your subject, drop the camera to a
lower level, and shoot up:

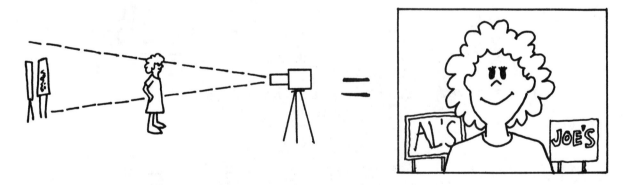

A LOWER CAMERA ANGLE REMOVES DISTRACTING ELEMENTS

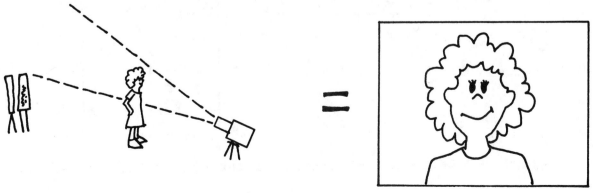

Another way to eliminate a distracting element in the background is to place either the subject or another object in the foreground to block the camera's view of the distracting element.

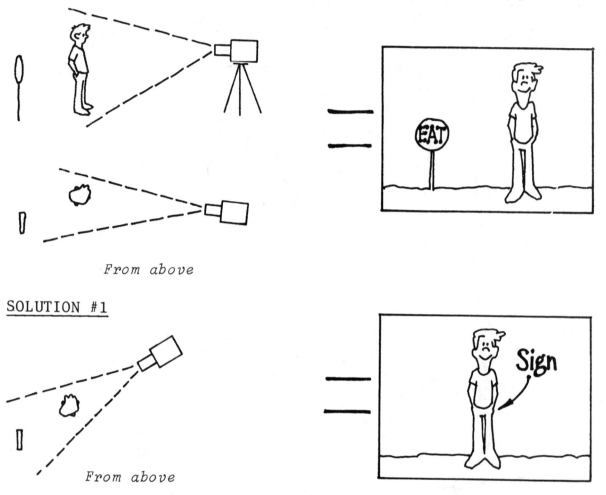

From above

SOLUTION #1

From above

The camera is moved around so that the man's body hides the sign in the background.

SOLUTION #2

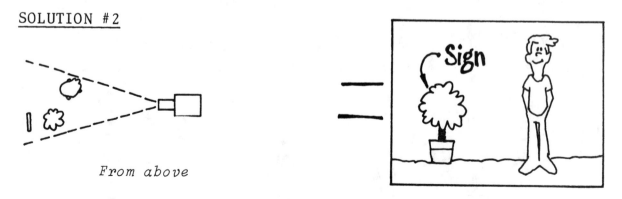

From above

A plant placed between the camera and the sign hides the sign.

IN SEARCH OF A GOOD COMPOSITION

A common mistake made by camerapersons everywhere is to arrive at a location, set up the camera in the first clear space that looks pretty good, and go from there. If you do this, you're short-changing yourself.

Sure, go ahead and set the camera down. But then take a quick walk around. As you walk, go up on your toes, squat down, lean from side to side. Find your best angle for framing, background, color, and balance. The whole operation could take less than a minute, and it's well worth your time. If you have trouble visualizing shots, carry the camera around with you and look through it to find your angle.

Remember, you don't have to accept the location exactly as you see it. If you've got a couple minutes, you can rearrange furniture, remove distracting elements, add interesting ones--do all kinds of things to improve your composition.

Look, then look again, as critically as you can. The human eye has a tendency to cancel out unimportant details, but the camera sees and records everything equally. Think back to that "perfect" shot of a wilderness sunset you took on vacation, only to discover when you picked up the prints that you had telephone wires running across the frame. When you learn to see the wires _before_ you take the picture, _then_ you can call yourself a cameraperson.

3. BASIC SEQUENCE

HOW A BASIC SEQUENCE WORKS

Look at this shot. Imagine that the man is talking to the boy.
Let's say he talks for thirty seconds. Try looking at the picture
while you count one-thousand-one, one-thousand-two, and so on, up
to thirty seconds.

If you're normal, you won't get much past one-thousand-ten
before your eyes start wandering. Now look at this sequence of
shots. Count to one-thousand-five at each one before moving to the
next.

1   2   3

4   5   6

That was a lot easier, wasn't it? So what have we proved? We've proved that it's easier to look at six different images in 30 seconds than to look at one single image for the same time. That's the idea behind the basic sequence--to break up one long scene into several shorter scenes. This makes the story more interesting for the viewer. It also gives us the opportunity, in editing, to vary the length and emphasis of the story as we desire. Let's review the basic sequence we've just seen, shot by shot, and see how it works.

WIDE SHOT

A WIDE SHOT or ESTABLISHING SHOT is simply that--a shot that's wide enough to establish your subject in the mind of the viewer. In this particular case, we see the man, the boy, and enough of their surroundings to establish that they're in the great outdoors.

Remember, a WIDE SHOT doesn't have to show everything--just everything that's important. A WIDE SHOT of a mountain would be a landscape. A WIDE SHOT of a man typing might show only the man and his computer, eliminating from the shot the rest of his desk and the surrounding office. A WIDE SHOT of an ant would be a fraction of an inch across.

MEDIUM SHOT

CLOSE-UP

The MEDIUM SHOT and the CLOSE-UP are, like the WIDE SHOT, endlessly variable, depending on your subject and your own point of view.

Essentially, the CLOSE-UP is the tightest, the closest you choose to be to your subject. In a person, it's usually a full head shot, as shown here. The MEDIUM SHOT falls somewhere in between the WIDE SHOT and the CLOSE-UP.

CUTAWAY

The CUTAWAY is the one shot that lets you easily change the length and/or order of your sequence. It's the shot most often forgotten by camerapersons and most often needed by editors.

In our sequence of the man and the boy, let's say that instead of talking for 30 seconds, the man talked for two minutes, the middle

minute-and-a-half of which was boring. So, in editing, you let the
man talk for the first 15 seconds, <u>cut away</u> to the boy listening,
throw out the boring middle of the talk, then cut back to the man
for the final 15 seconds. So instead of this:

we have this:

The splice in the sound track between Scenes 1 and 6 is covered
by the cutaway of the boy listening.

The most common cutaway is the shot of the reporter listening
in TV interviews. However, anything can serve as a cutaway, as long

as it's related to the main action, but not visually connected to it. That's the great value of a cutaway: when you cut to it, you don't have to match anything in the main shot you're cutting away from.

For example, a sequence of a man making toys can be shortened or rearranged by cutting away to shots of already completed toys on the shelves. Or the toymaker's face can serve as a cutaway from close-up actions of his hands working on the toy.

If you look hard enough, you can find a cutaway for just about any sequence you shoot. In an interview with an athlete, his photos and trophies are cutaways. If a woman is just sitting and talking to the camera, a close-up of her hands in her lap is a cutaway. An extreme wide shot, or a shot from behind, can also be a cutaway.

Cutaways can serve to enhance the story. If a man is talking about how he won an auto race, you can cut away to footage of the race, while continuing his voice on the sound track. If an interviewee mentions a person who helped her in her career, you can cut away to a shot of that person.

SHOOTING A BASIC SEQUENCE

The most important thing to remember in shooting a basic sequence is that EACH NEW SHOT SHOULD, IF AT ALL POSSIBLE, INVOLVE A CHANGE IN BOTH IMAGE SIZE AND CAMERA ANGLE. This not only makes the sequence more interesting but, as we'll see, it makes it much easier to cut back and forth between shots. On the following page is a diagram, from above, showing where I placed the camera for the sequence of the man talking to the boy.

48

CAMERA SET-UP - BASIC SEQUENCE

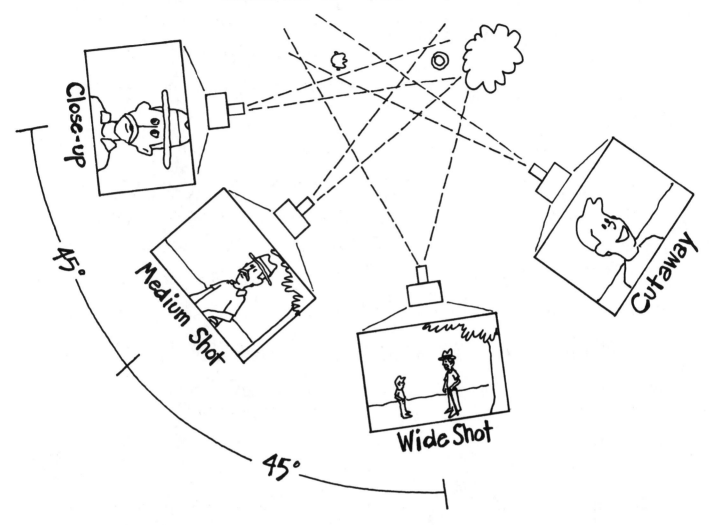

Notice that between WIDE SHOT, MEDIUM SHOT, and CLOSE-UP, I changed my camera angle by at least 45 degrees. You should always try to move your camera at least that much.

It's pretty obvious that a change in image size and angle between shots makes for a more interesting sequence. What's not quite so obvious is that it makes the transition from shot to shot smoother and easier to accomplish. With rare exceptions, most non-studio work is shot with a single camera. This means your subject has to repeat himself for the medium shots and close-ups. He's not always going to be able to remember and duplicate his actions exactly for every take. So you might end up having to cut from a wide shot

where he's looking straight ahead

to a medium shot where his head is inclined slightly downward:

If you change image size and not camera angle, you'll see the man's

head jerk down on the cut. This is called a jump cut.

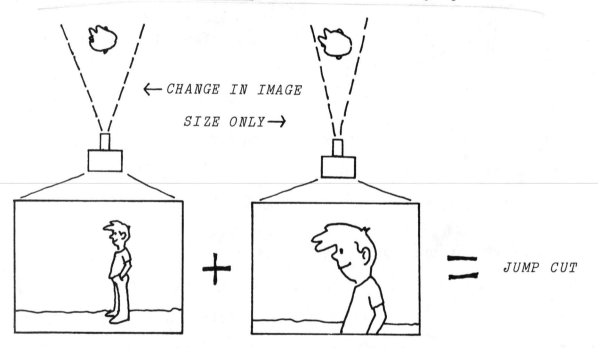

← CHANGE IN IMAGE

SIZE ONLY →

JUMP CUT

But, if you change not only the image size but also the camera

angle, you'll be home free. The combination of image change and

angle change will alter the viewer's perspective just enough for him not to notice the slight mismatch in head position.

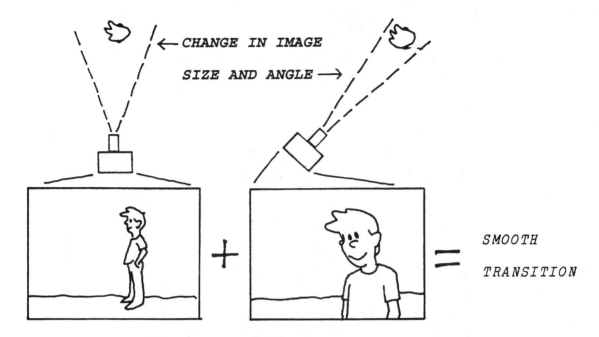

CHANGE IN IMAGE SIZE AND ANGLE →

SMOOTH
TRANSITION

Often, you'll find that a change in image size and camera
angle will cover even greater mismatches.

One special situation: When your subject is talking directly to
the camera and you change camera angles, be sure to show the subject
physically pivoting his body from one camera position to the other.
Otherwise, the abrupt change in background will confuse the viewer.
If you prefer, in the editing, you can cut on the action of the turn.
They do this every night on your local news show when the anchor
turns to a new camera and says "On the local scene...".

CUTTING ON THE ACTION

A good way to get smooth transitions between shots is to cut
on the action. The viewer's eye naturally follows movement on the
screen. If a movement begins in one shot and ends in the next, the
viewer's eye will follow the action right across the cut, without
paying much attention to anything else.

Let's say that the man in our original basic sequence takes off
his hat. We shoot the wide shot down to the point where he completes the action of removing his hat. Then we set the camera up
for the medium shot, and have him begin the medium shot by repeating
the action of removing his hat.

WIDE SHOT   MEDIUM SHOT

Then, in the editing, we CUT ON THE ACTION, so that he starts removing his hat in the wide shot and completes the removal in the
medium shot. Without even realizing it, the viewer is carried
smoothly from one shot to the next.

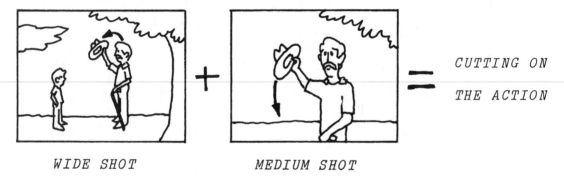

WIDE SHOT   MEDIUM SHOT

CUTTING ON

THE ACTION

There are lots of obvious situations where it's convenient to
cut on the action. For example: opening doors, getting out of cars,
sitting down, standing up, reaching for objects, walking, running,
jumping--almost any kind of movement. The important thing to remember is that the last action of the first shot has to be repeated at
the beginning of the second shot. So you have to shoot the same
movement twice. This is called overlapping action.

CLEAN ENTRANCE - CLEAN EXIT

Having a clean entrance and a clean exit is almost as good as having a million different cutaways. Clean entrances and exits give you terrific flexibility in your editing. Let's say for example that you are shooting an explanation of the controls on a complicated piece of equipment. Your master shot--the one where you keep the camera running for the whole explanation--looks like this:

As the man explains the different buttons, he touches them and turns them. When you've finished the master shot, move in for close-ups of the different knobs. Start each shot showing only the knob on the machine. Then have the man's hand come in (CLEAN ENTRANCE), fiddle with the knob, and go out again (CLEAN EXIT), leaving once more just the knob in the frame.

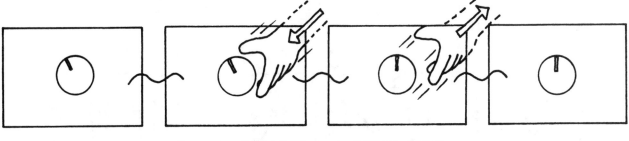

CLEAN ENTRANCE   *CLEAN EXIT*

So what does this do for us? Well, first off, if you cut to the knob, wait a beat, then have the hand enter, you don't have to

worry about matching the position of the man's hand from the wide
shot to the close-up, because when you cut to the close-up the hand
isn't yet in the frame.

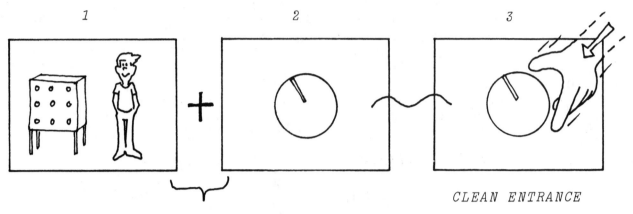

NOTHING HAS TO MATCH

OVER THIS CUT

CLEAN ENTRANCE

Secondly, let's say you decide after the shoot that you only
have time to explain the most important controls and you're going
to have to eliminate some of the middle explanations. Easy as pie.
Just go to a close-up of the last knob before the section you want
to eliminate, let the hand exit cleanly, wait a beat, then cut to
the wide shot, picking it up after the dropped section. Since
you're cutting from a close-up of the knob without the hand, nothing
has to match when you go back to the wide shot at a much later point
in the explanation.

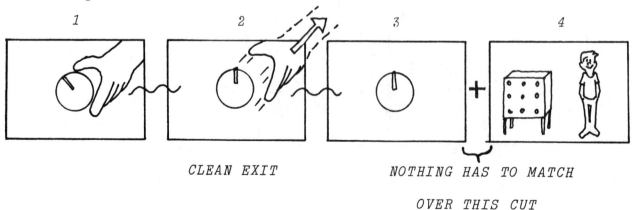

CLEAN EXIT

NOTHING HAS TO MATCH

OVER THIS CUT

If you think about it, you can see there are many ways this sequence could be rearranged by taking advantage of the clean entrances and exits of the hand.

Let's look at another example. Say you've got a wide shot of a car driving by and you have to cut to a different shot of the same car, but the background is different. If you just cut from one shot to the other, the change in backgrounds will be very noticeable. But, if you let the car exit the frame in the first shot, hold a beat, then cut to the new shot with a different background, it'll work. By not see-ing the car for a second or two, the audience will accept that it had time to get to a different place for the following shot.

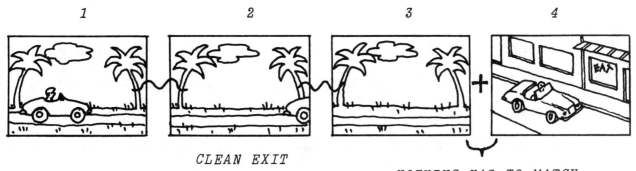

CLEAN EXIT

NOTHING HAS TO MATCH

OVER THIS CUT

Or you could accomplish the same thing by cutting to the new shot without the car there, waiting a beat, and then letting the car make a clean entrance.

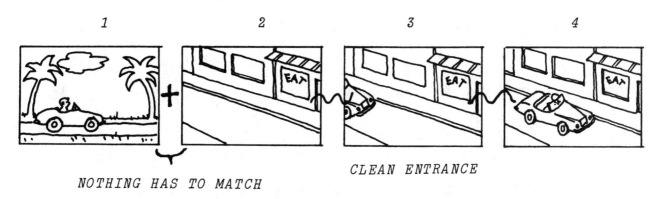

NOTHING HAS TO MATCH

OVER THIS CUT

CLEAN ENTRANCE

Clean entrances and clean exits are very helpful in getting people quickly from one place to another. Say you have a sequence of a boy walking into his house and upstairs to his room. Rather than follow him all the way up with the camera, just show him walking in the front door (CLEAN EXIT), then cut to his room as he enters it (CLEAN ENTRANCE).

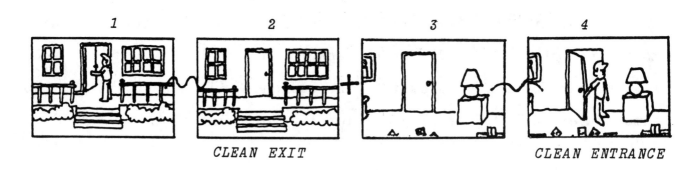

CLEAN EXIT   CLEAN ENTRANCE

Clean entrances and exits are good for almost any kind of shot where somebody or something is moving from one place to another, picking something up, putting something down, hitting, pulling, selecting, etc. Whenever you have anything moving through your frame, particularly in a close-up, you'll be doing yourself a big favor by giving it either a clean entrance or a clean exit, or both. This will always allow you greater freedom in your editing.

SOME FINAL WORDS ON BASIC SEQUENCES

Only amateurs and some geniuses plan on making every cut a match cut. The more you cover yourself with changes in image size, changes in camera angle, cutaways, overlapping actions, and clean entrances and clean exits, the better your final product will be.

Remember, any still photographer can shoot a bunch of pretty shots, but only a real cameraperson can shoot a sequence.

4. SCREEN DIRECTION

SCREEN DIRECTION AND CROSSING THE LINE

Screen direction is the direction people and things face when viewed through the camera.

Have you ever been watching a conversation on TV between two people when suddenly the scene changes and it looks like one of them is talking to the back of the other's head? That's called reversed screen direction. The cameraperson causes it by CROSSING THE LINE.

The line is also known as the axis of action, or simply the axis. By whatever name, it's an imaginary line which determines the direction people and things face when viewed through the camera. When you cross the line, you reverse the screen direction of everything you see through the camera, even though nothing has moved but the camera.

In our sequence of the man talking to the boy, the line would intersect the man and the boy.

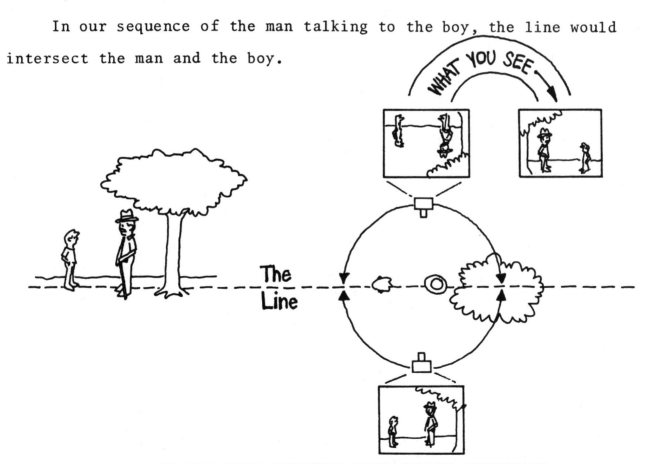

CROSSING THE LINE REVERSES YOUR SCREEN DIRECTION

As long as the camera stays on the front side of the line, the man will be looking screen left and the boy will be looking screen right. If you cross the line, they'll be looking in just the opposite directions, although they haven't moved at all. Now, this is really no problem, as long as you stay on one side of the line or the other. But you can't go jumping back and forth.

Say you make your wide shot from one side of the line, like this:

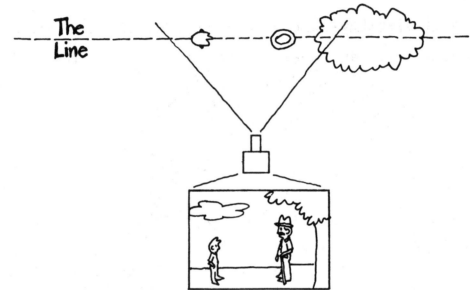

Then, for some reason, you shoot your cutaway of the boy from the other side, like this:

When you cut them together, you get this:

It looks like the boy has turned completely around, with his back to the man!

Let's take another example, a person working at a computer. See what happens when you cross the line.

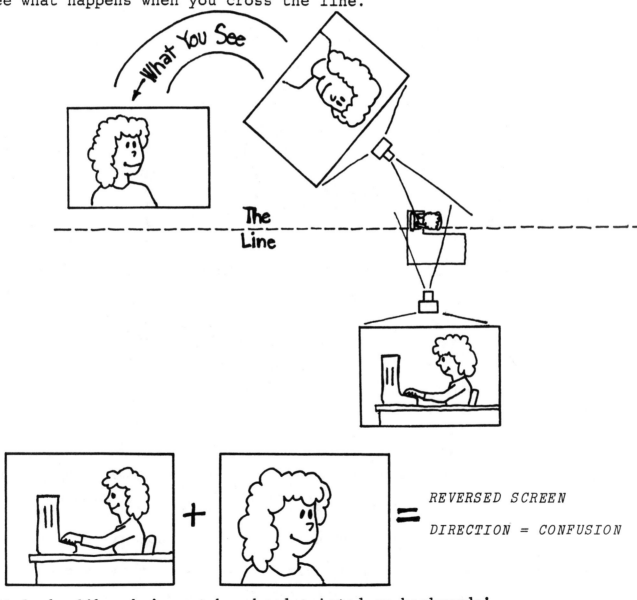

It looks like she's got her head twisted on backwards!

There are circumstances in which you have to cross the line, whether you want to or not. Maybe your subject's body is blocking a new detail you need to show. Maybe part of your sequence just looks better from the other side of the line. Maybe you have no control over your subject's movements. Whatever, don't fear. There <u>are</u> ways to cross the line without confusing your viewer.

The easiest way is when your subject changes direction on camera, within the frame. You stand still, and the line actually crosses under you. For example, a car turning around. Or a person turning from a friend on his right to a friend on his left. As long as the change in screen direction is made on camera, there's no confusion.

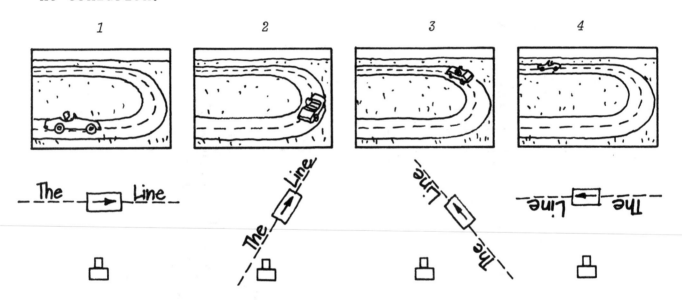

CROSSING THE LINE - SUBJECT CHANGES DIRECTION ON CAMERA

Another way is to cross the line in one continuous move with the camera. In uncontrolled situations, this is sometimes your only recourse. Say a race car mechanic is working on a car and he moves so you can't see what he's doing. All you can do, if you want the shot, is to keep the camera running and walk around to where you can see what's going on:

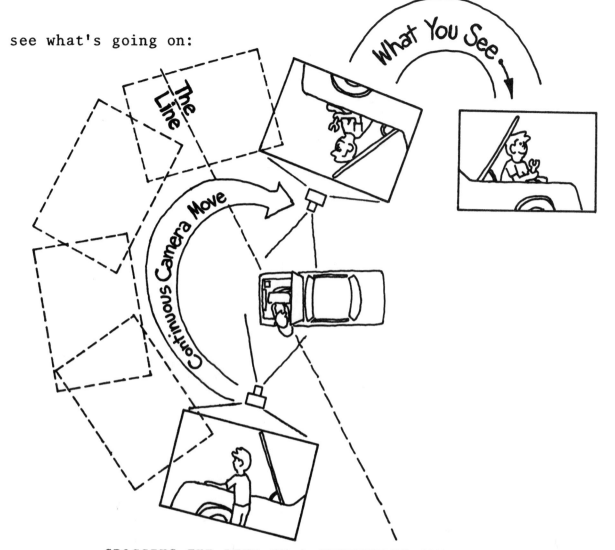

CROSSING THE LINE IN A CONTINUOUS CAMERA MOVE

You see this type of shot frequently in TV commercials and feature films. It's usually done with a dolly--a camera platform on wheels.

Sooner or later we all get in a situation where we're finishing up shooting a sequence and we know we've jumped back and forth across the line. No matter what the reason, we've got to figure some way to save the day. This is where my favorite line-crossing method comes in handy. It's based on a simple truth: YOU CAN CROSS THE LINE IF YOU STOP ON IT. You can go from one screen direction to another if you put a neutral shot with no screen direction in the middle. As long as you have at least one neutral shot as a bridge, you can cross the line.

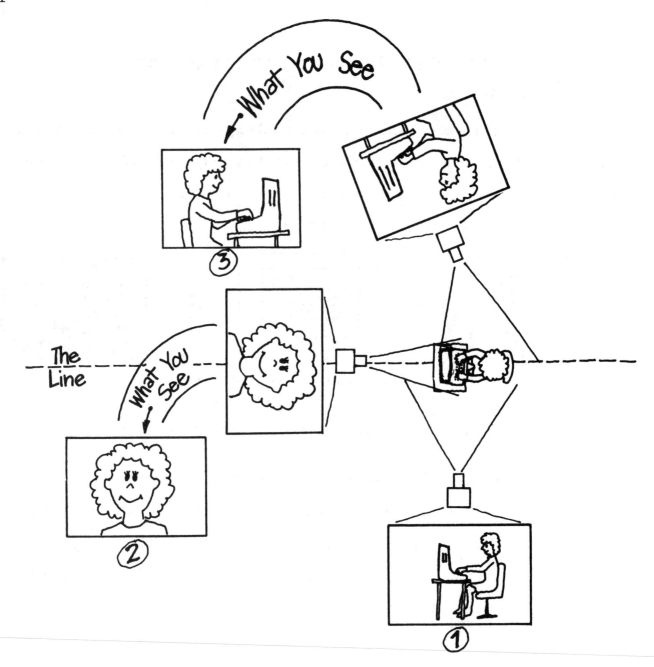

NEUTRAL SHOT ON THE LINE
- NO SCREEN DIRECTION -

YOU CAN CROSS THE LINE IF YOU STOP ON IT

You'd be amazed at the mileage you can get out of one or two good neutral shots.

One neutral shot which doesn't always occur to everybody is the POV, the point-of-view shot. In the sequence of the woman typing, the point-of-view would be a shot of the computer screen from the point of view of the typist.

POINT-OF-VIEW ON THE LINE
- NO SCREEN DIRECTION -

CROSSING THE LINE WITH A POINT-OF-VIEW SHOT

Often you can fake a point-of-view shot after your subject has left. For the closeup of the computer screen, who says you have to use the same person, if you don't see her hands in the shot? Or, if you need to show hands, you can still use another woman with similar hands.

There are two other ways to cross the line which, though not perfect, are certainly better than nothing.

First is the situation where you have a clean point of reference to help the viewer orient himself a little. In a lot of old movies, you'll see a wide shot of people going up a gangplank to a ship, followed by a medium shot from across the line. The argument here is that the gangplank serves as a reference for the audience to hold onto.

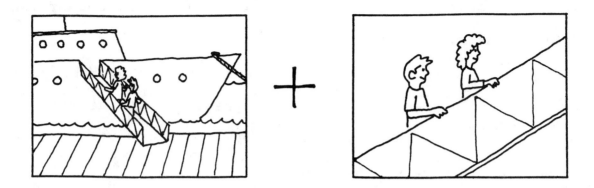

CROSSING THE LINE WITH A REFERENCE

Other common references which can ease a reversal in screen direction are sidewalks, roads, hallways, tables, cars, boats-- anything that's in both shots and has a clearly defined direction of its own. Please note: this does not make a perfect cut, but it's better than nothing.

The other not-so-perfect way to reverse screen direction is to cross the line at the same time as you cut on the action. The idea is that the continuity of action over the cut will psychologically cover the reversal in screen direction.

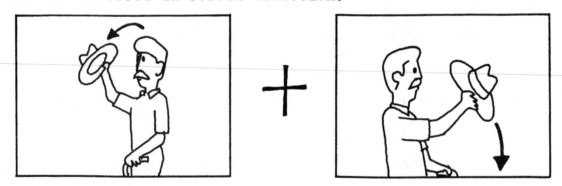

CROSSING THE LINE BY CUTTING ON THE ACTION

Again, it's not perfect. But in a pinch, it's better than nothing.

USING SCREEN DIRECTION TO SOLVE SHOOTING PROBLEMS

As we learned earlier, screen direction is the direction people and things face when viewed through the camera. It's determined by the axis of action, the line. When you cross the line, you reverse your screen direction, even though nothing has moved but the camera. The corollary to this is: AS LONG AS YOU DON'T CROSS THE LINE, AS LONG AS YOU KEEP THE SAME SCREEN DIRECTION, YOU CAN MOVE PEOPLE, THINGS AND CAMERA ANYWHERE YOU WANT. This can help you solve many shooting problems.

Let's say you're shooting an interview with a well-known naturalist. Since he'll be talking about the wonders of the great outdoors, it would look best if he were in an outdoorsy setting. But for reasons of time and money, you have to shoot in his suburban backyard. After a quick reconnoiter of the backyard, you find your best location and select two camera positions:

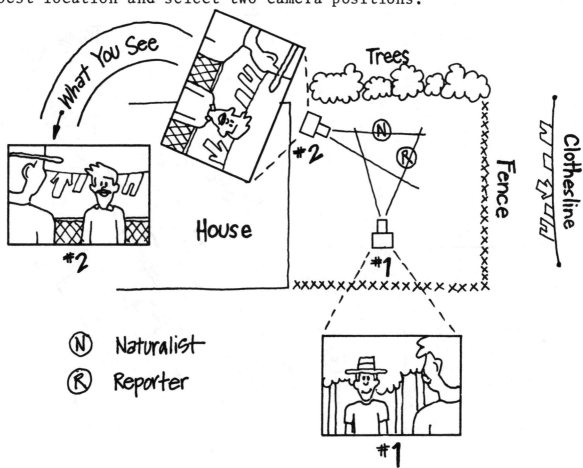

From Position #1, you can do your wide shot over the shoulder of the reporter, as well as medium shots and close-ups of the naturalist--all with lush trees in the background. So far, so good. But, when you move around to Position #2 for your shots of the reporter, you see an ugly fence and the neighbor's clothesline in the background. Not exactly the lush natural setting you'd like.

MISMATCHED BACKGROUNDS.
#2'S BACKGROUND DISTRACTS
FROM CONTENT OF INTERVIEW.

The solution? After you've finished with all of your shots of the naturalist from Position #1, pivot the naturalist and the reporter counter-clockwise so that the trees are now behind the reporter, <u>who is still facing screen left.</u>

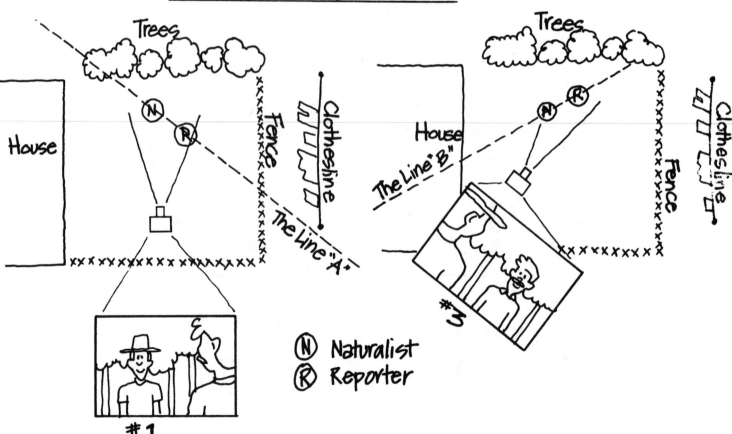

You see, you haven't crossed the line. You've merely pivoted it--and your subjects--from Position A to Position B. As long as you stay on the same side of the line and keep the same screen direction, you can move the line anywhere you want. In fact, in a pinch, you could even shoot the reporter's close-ups--without the naturalist--at another place and time!

MATCHED BACKGROUNDS,
CONTRIBUTE TO CONTENT
OF INTERVIEW.

Ah hah, you might say. It still won't work because we <u>know</u> there's a fence behind the reporter and not trees. Well, maybe <u>we</u> know it, but the viewer sure doesn't. All he knows is what he sees on the screen. Screen geography has nothing to do with real geography. <u>Nothing exists for the viewer except what you show him.</u> Once you understand this, you can work wonders.

You won't always have to go the extremes illustrated by this example. Sometimes it's just a matter of moving or pivoting your subject a few feet one way or the other to get a better shot. Remember, as long as you keep the same screen direction and everything else matches, you've got nothing to worry about. I've moved people closer to windows to get better light on close-ups, put them in different rooms to get better backgrounds; once, in a very tight situation, I shot five different angles without moving the camera, but moving the subjects instead--and it worked!

5. CAMERA MOVES

WHY CAMERA MOVES?

There's a tendency among camerapersons, especially beginners, to be continually moving the camera--zooming in, zooming out, panning left, panning right, tilting up, tilting down. I guess they feel they're not earning their money if they just hold the camera still. They're wrong. A camera move should have a purpose. It should in some way contribute to the viewer's understanding of what he's seeing. If it doesn't, the move distracts and calls attention to itself.

Camera moves limit you in your editing. If the only shot you have of a certain subject is a zoom and the zoom lasts 15 seconds, but you only have 5 seconds of narration to go over it, you're stuck. Either you leave the whole move in, and your viewers sit bored for ten seconds of silence, or you cut in and out of a five-second piece of the zoom, which is visually jarring. The safe thing to do is shoot your move, then cover yourself with a couple of static shots of the same thing. You'll be glad you did when you start editing.

The basic camera moves are ZOOMS, PANS, TILTS, and combinations thereof.

In general, a ZOOM-IN (from wide shot to close-up) directs our attention to whatever it is we're zooming in on. So if you zoom in, try to zoom in on something interesting or important.

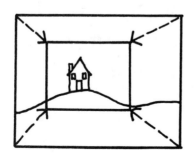

A ZOOM-IN DIRECTS ATTENTION

A ZOOM-OUT (from close-up to wide shot) usually reveals new information. Often it tells us where we are. For example, you can start on a close-up of a man's face talking about flowers, then zoom back to reveal that he's surrounded by flowers.

A ZOOM-OUT REVEALS NEW INFORMATION

PANS (horizontal moves) and TILTS (vertical moves) also reveal new information.

PANS AND TILTS REVEAL NEW INFORMATION

One caution about pans. If you pan too fast, vertical lines, like fenceposts, doorframes, etc., will strobe on you, trailing ghost images behind. When in doubt, pan a little slower.

An effective way to lead your viewer through a long pan is to follow a smaller object--a person walking, a car perhaps--as it passes by your subject. For example, a wide shot pan across the front of a building is much more interesting with a person walking by, leading the move.

MAKING CAMERA MOVES

The first rule of camera movement is this: BEGIN AND END
EVERY MOVE WITH A WELL-COMPOSED STATIC SHOT. It's very distracting
to cut from a static composition to a move that's already in
progress. Likewise, to cut from a move to a static. Oh, you can
do it, and sometimes it works when you want to create a feeling of
excitement and action. And you _can_ dissolve between static shots
and moves, visually blending one scene into another, with good
results. But why limit your options? If you're going to make a
move, hold it steady for a beat or two at the beginning, ease into
your move, make the move, ease gradually out of the move, and hold
for a beat or two at the end. You'll be glad you did when you
start editing.

BEGIN AND END EVERY MOVE WITH A WELL-COMPOSED STATIC SHOT

The other rule of camera movement is this: ALWAYS MOVE FROM
AN UNCOMFORTABLE POSITION TO A COMFORTABLE POSITION. This is especially important in pans, when you're moving in a wide horizontal
arc. Have you ever seen a cameraperson start to pan with a passing
car and, as he follows the car by, slowly twist himself into a
quivering pretzel? He's starting with his muscles relaxed and
then twisting them into a tense, unnatural position. For the
smoothest possible move, he should be doing just the opposite. He
should get comfortable in his end position, then twist around into
the beginning position. That way, when he makes the move, his

muscles will be relaxing, untensing, returning smoothly to their
natural position. He'll be moving from uncomfortable to comfortable,
smoothly, naturally. This is true of any move, not just pans.

MOVE FROM UNCOMFORTABLE TO COMFORTABLE

One final tip. I've found that when combining a zoom with a
tilt or a pan, it works smoother if I start the pan or tilt just a
fraction of a second before the zoom. I don't know why it works
better this way, but it does.

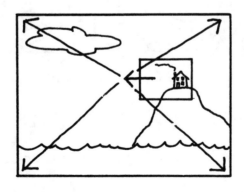

ON COMBINED MOVES, START THE PAN OR TILT A FRACTION OF A
SECOND BEFORE THE ZOOM.

71

6. MONTAGES

A montage is a series of related shots used to condense time or distance, set a mood, or summarize information. For example, a montage of highway signs, a montage of pretty nature shots, or a montage of company products. Most TV commercials are montages.

For a montage to work, it's usually best if each shot is clearly different from the one before it; otherwise it looks like a bad cut between two similar shots of the same thing. If you shoot an employee montage with everybody framed the same, it will look like one face changing abruptly into another. But if you shoot a variety of angles and image sizes, the effect can be very nice.

AN INEFFECTIVE MONTAGE - THE SHOTS ARE TOO SIMILAR

AN EFFECTIVE MONTAGE - EACH SHOT IS DIFFERENT

An easy way to make a nice sign montage is to tilt each one a different way. For some reason these are called Dutch tilts.

7. LIGHTING

EXTERIOR LIGHTING

The most powerful and common source of light is the sun, but for film and TV it has one big disadvantage: it's always moving. It traces an arc across the sky, east to west, horizon to horizon, every day. This means that the angle at which sunlight is falling on our subjects is also constantly changing. Most people look their best in sunlight when the sun is no higher than about 45° above the horizon. When the sun is higher, around the noon hour, it casts ugly shadows on faces. Eye sockets go dark and little shadow "beards" show up on chins and under cheekbones and noses.

PEOPLE LOOK BEST IN SUNLIGHT FALLING AT ANGLES OF 45 DEGREES OR LESS. THE NOONTIME OVERHEAD SUN CASTS UGLY SHADOWS.

Most exterior shots are made with the subject facing the sun, so it illuminates him directly. Sometimes, though, this isn't possible or desirable. Perhaps the location doesn't permit it; or maybe the sun is bothering your subject's eyes; or maybe your subject looks really nice with the sun behind him. So you end up shooting with backlight or sidelight. Both conditions cast strong shadows on your subject's face.

SIDELIGHT AND BACKLIGHT CAST STRONG SHADOWS

The shadows cast by backlight and sidelight can be filled in--
brightened up with light--in two ways: reflectors and fill lights.

A reflector is anything which reflects light. It's normally
a board covered with silver paint or foil. But it can also be a
white poster board, or a white wall, or a piece of canvas. You use
the reflector to bounce sunlight into the shadow areas where it's
needed.

REFLECTORS FILL IN SHADOW AREAS WITH BOUNCED SUNLIGHT

Any light can be used as a fill light outside, as long as it
puts out daylight-colored light, with a color temperature of 5400K.
The lamp can be 5400K; or it can be 3200K-tungsten, with a dichroic
filter or a blue gelatin sheet in front to convert it to 5400K.

One disadvantage to using a fill light instead of a reflector
is that you need electricity to power it--from a battery, a portable
generator, or an extension cord. Another disadvantage is that, in
order to match the tremendous brightness of the sun, you either have
to bring the fill light in very close to the subject; or else use
a very powerful fill light, requiring a lot of electricity.

The advantage to a fill light is that, unlike a reflector, it's
not directly dependent on the sun. You can place it anywhere you
want, at any angle you want, for the best lighting effect and for
maximum comfort of your subject. The fill light is especially useful in completely backlit situations where a reflector may shine a
glare right into your subject's eyes.

A FILL LIGHT BRIGHTENS UP SHADOW AREAS REGARDLESS OF WHERE THE SUN IS.

A fill light is the best way to brighten up the shadows cast by the noontime overhead sun. And on overcast days, a light shining directly on your subject can stand in for an absent sun and give your pictures needed brightness and contrast.

INTERIOR LIGHTING

There are three basic types of lights used most frequently in interior lighting: focusing quartz, broads, and softlights.

The focusing quartz light is the movie and TV version of the theatrical spot light. It's the most common, versatile light in use. By moving a lever, you control the intensity and pattern of light it puts out. The range is from "spot" to "flood." At "spot," you get a small, concentrated area of light. At "flood," you get a spread-out, less intense area.

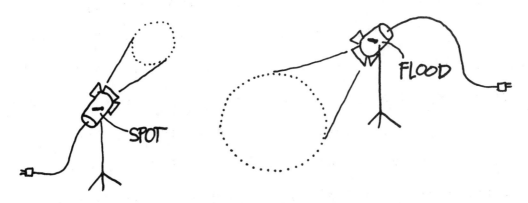

FOCUSING QUARTZ LIGHTS RANGE FROM SPOT TO FLOOD.

One caution on using focusing quartz lights: don't count on getting a smooth even pattern of light at every setting. Even at full flood you may find a hot spot or two. Before doing any really critical lighting, your best bet is to shine each light on the wall or the floor and run it through the whole range from spot to flood, noticing the light pattern at each setting.

Quartz lights, even on flood, put out a hard, direct light. This produces sharp-edged dark shadows, which are not always desirable, especially in people shots. To diffuse the light--to spread it out and produce softer, more flattering shadows--we can do one of two things: either put diffusing material, like spun glass, in front of the light; or bounce the light off a reflector-type surface, like a white wall or ceiling, or a silver-coated space blanket taped to the ceiling. Both methods work well, but they also reduce the amount of light reaching the subject.

QUARTZ LIGHT CAN BE SOFTENED BY DIFFUSION MATERIAL IN FRONT OF THE LIGHT, OR BY BOUNCING THE LIGHT OFF A RE-FLECTOR-TYPE SURFACE.

Broads are non-focusing lights designed to put out a broad even light over a large area. They have no fine-tuning controls. All you do is turn them on and point them. The hard, direct light from a broad, like that from a focusing quartz, can be softened with diffusion material or by bouncing.

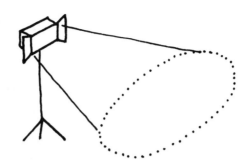

A BROAD LIGHT PUTS OUT A FLAT EVEN PATTERN OF LIGHT

A <u>softlight</u> is a permanent, portable bounce light. It consists
of a curved scoop, the inside of which is white or silver-colored.
A broad-type lamp is mounted facing the scoop, so that its light
bounces off the curved surface and out towards the subject.

A SOFTLIGHT IS A PERMANENT, PORTABLE BOUNCE LIGHT

The advantages of a softlight over a bounced light are con-
venience--you can use it anywhere, with no need for a wall or ceiling
to bounce off--and control--it's easier to direct the light exactly
where you want it. However, it does take up more space.

Most lights, be they focusing, broads or softlights, come with
barn doors. These are little black flaps which are used to block
off light from areas where you don't want it, to shape the pattern
of light you put out. They are very useful.

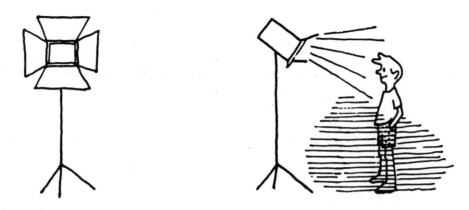

BARN DOORS SHAPE THE PATTERN OF LIGHT

BASIC LIGHTING SET-UP

The classic basic lighting set-up is as follows:

First you place your key light to one side of the camera and at about a 45° angle above your subject. This is your main light, the basis for the rest of your lighting set-up.

Unless you have a good reason, no area in your frame should be brighter than the area lit by the key light. The viewer's eye is always attracted first to the brightest area of the frame. If that turns out to be the background, then your lighting isn't working the way it should; or it's working in a special way, which you should be aware of.

Set up your fill light on the opposite side of the subject from the key light. The fill should be bright enough to partially fill in the shadows from the key, leaving just enough shadows on the subject's face to give a feeling of depth. (Completely shadowless lighting is called flat lighting and gives less sense of depth.)

*KEY LIGHT ALONE = HEAVY
SHADOWS*

*KEY + FILL = JUST ENOUGH
SHADOWS FOR FEELING OF DEPTH*

Next, place your backlight. This falls on your subject's head and shoulders from behind, creating a rim of light which visually separates him from the background. The backlight is especially useful when the subject's hair or clothes are similar in color to the background.

THE BACKLIGHT SEPARATES THE SUBJECT FROM THE BACKGROUND.

Last but not least, place your background light. This brings the background up into the same range of illumination as the rest of the scene and gives an added sense of depth. As a general rule, it's a good idea to have your background a little darker than your key area.

Well, you say, so now I know how to light one person. But how do I light two or three or more? And what happens if they start moving around? Well, you multiply the basic set-up. You place a key light for every important area, then start building. It gets complicated, but if you just take it one step at a time you'll do all right.

Often you'll find you can cover more than one subject with the same key light. Or that the fall-off from one subject's key light can serve as fill light on another subject. A single broad can provide backlight for several people.

To avoid multiple, unnatural-looking shadows on walls, keep your lights high and your subjects away from the walls. Keep in mind that shadows are less noticeable on dark-colored walls than on light-colored ones; so, sometimes a change of scenery can solve a lighting problem. Also, film shows more shadow detail than video; so for TV, you'll have to throw more light into your shadow areas.

In the last few years, a lot of camerapersons--myself included--have begun lighting entire scenes with bounce light. It's not dramatic lighting; but it _is_ quick and efficient, and it looks natural in a lot of situations.

Really good lighting for TV and film is an art in itself. Please don't take the basic lighting set-up as gospel. Like the rule of thirds in composition, it's a place to start--no more, no less.

The best advice I can give you for your first few lighting jobs is to be methodical. Go slow. Put up one light at a time and watch what it does. If you do get confused at some point, turn off all your lights. Then turn them on again one at a time, so you can see what each is doing and regain control.

8. DOING IT

PLANNING AND SHOOTING A SEQUENCE

When planning a shoot, the first thing is to decide what you want to end up with. What sort of story do you want to tell? Who will be your audience? How do you want them to react? What things should you emphasize? What should you downplay? Keep all this in mind as you look over the location and talk with the people you'll be working with.

Next, make a shooting plan, even if it's only in your head. Decide where your camera and subjects will be for each shot. For relatively short sequences, your best bet is to shoot the whole thing all the way through in a wide shot; then repeat it in a medium shot, and again in a close-up. Then shoot your cutaways. This method uses up a lot of tape or film, but you can be sure you'll have material for editing. It's probably the best way to shoot your first few projects.

Later, after you have a better understanding of what you're doing, you can try shooting all the way through in a wide shot, and then just repeating certain sections for medium shots, close-ups and cutaways. At this stage of the game, you'll have to start thinking about slates.

A slate is simply a piece of identification, whether on a fancy clapboard or a scrap of paper. When you have many different shots to piece together in the editing, you need some way to quickly tell one from the other. That's what slates are for. You write a scene number or a description on the slate, hold it in front of the camera, and run off a second or two of it before you shoot the scene.

81

Slates are wonderful things. They never forget, even if you do.
Any time you have the slightest doubt that the editor might not
know what a scene is or where it goes, tell him with a slate. You
should do this even if you're going to edit everything yourself. In
the first place, it's good discipline. It forces you to think about
how the pieces are going to fit together. Secondly, who wants to
spend half an editing session wondering where this scene goes or
where that one goes, when a simple slate could tell you in a second?
Also, if you number various takes of the same scene, you can go im-
mediately to the one marked best on your location notes, and not
waste time reviewing bad takes.

SHOOTING SCRIPTS AND STORYBOARDS

Often it helps to make up a <u>shooting script.</u> This is simply a
list of what you're going to shoot and how you're going to shoot it.
For example:

VIDEO	*AUDIO*
1. WIDE SHOT. Salesman by car.	SALESMAN: Hiya folks! Let me tell you about the new Zootmobile!
2. MEDIUM SHOT. Salesman. PAN as he moves to sticker on window.	This car is the greatest! And cheap? I'll tell you it's cheap! Look at this sticker!
3. CLOSE-UP. Sticker	25,000 drachmas! And that's including tax, tag and dealer prep!
4. WIDE SHOT. Salesman by car.	So come on down and buy one today! Okay? Okay!

Sometimes you can visualize better what you're going to shoot
if you make up a storyboard. A storyboard is a series of simple
drawings--you can do them with stick figures--representing the shots
you plan to make. Drawing a storyboard is like a free practice
shoot--and it doesn't use up any film or tape! For example:

1

Hiya folks! Let me tell you
about the new Zootmobile!

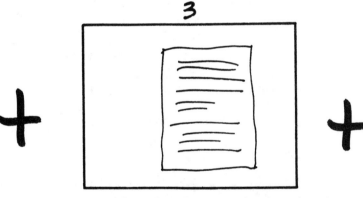

2a

This car is the greatest! And
cheap? I'll tell you it's cheap!

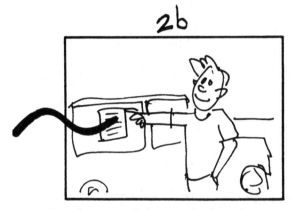

2b

Look at this sticker!

3

25,000 drachmas! And that's in-
cluding tax, tag and dealer prep!

4

So come on down and buy one
today! Okay? Okay!

SHOOTING OUT OF SEQUENCE

For some sequences, especially those involving a lot of lighting changes, there are advantages to shooting the scenes out of sequence-out of order.

Say, for example, that only the first 30 seconds and the last 15 seconds of your sequence need to be shown in a wide shot. What you do is, set up for your wide shot, shoot the first 30 seconds, cut, then jump ahead and shoot the last 15 seconds right then, without moving the camera. This way you're finished once and for all with that camera position. Now you can move your lights, microphones and everything else around for your other shots. And you don't have to worry about putting everything back again for the end wide shot-because you've already shot it!

Take another example. Say you have a sequence consisting of four scenes. You decide that Scenes 1 and 3 will be shot from Camera Position A. Scenes 2 and 4 will look best from Position B. If you have control of the situation, it makes a lot more sense to shoot Scene 1 from Position A, stay there and shoot Scene 3; and then move to Position B for Scenes 2 and 4. That way you move the camera one time. If you shoot the scenes in their natural order, you'll move the camera three times: From A for Scene 1 to B for Scene 2 to A for Scene 3 to B for Scene 4.

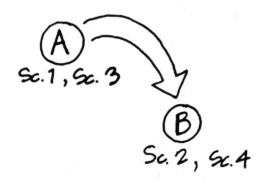

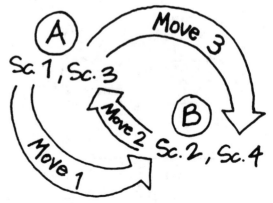

OUT OF SEQUENCE
ONE CAMERA MOVE

IN SEQUENCE
THREE CAMERA MOVES

When circumstances allow, you can save a lot of time and energy by shooting out of sequence. Just remember to plan well, and don't forget your slates!

COMMUNICATING

Everybody has his or her own philosophy of working. I'd like to make a small pitch for mine.

I believe in communicating. I try to let everybody, from my assistants to the people who will appear on camera, know what we're going to do. Before we start, I discuss the shooting plan, ask for suggestions, and let everybody look through the camera. I try to get across the idea that we're all on the same team and we're going to have fun. Most of the time, we do.

Of course, I also make it understood that, for the shoot to go smoothly, somebody has to be in charge--and that somebody is me. But since by this point everybody knows what we're doing and why, mine can usually be a benevolent dictatorship.

WORKING IN UNCONTROLLED SITUATIONS

Sooner or later you'll find yourself working in a totally un-controlled situation. If you're a television news cameraperson, you'll be doing it every day. But you can still use what you've learned in this book.

You can always try for a decent composition. You can construct basic sequences by regularly changing your camera angle and image size, and by grabbing cutaways wherever you can--even if it's the old standby of a closeup of another cameraperson. You can maintain your screen direction--and cover yourself with neutral shots when you cross the line. You can let your subject enter and exit the frame cleanly. You can still shoot great sequences--you just have to hustle more to get them.

Shooting in uncontrolled situations can be exciting and fun, especially when it's all over and you know that in spite of everything you've got footage that works.

SOME FINAL WORDS

Making moving pictures is a subjective art. There are no absolute rights and wrongs. But there <u>are</u> some things that usually work—like the things I've explained to you in this book.

If you want to stray from the basics, fine. Just be sure you understand what you're doing and why; otherwise you lose control of your work and confuse your viewers. Until you're really sure of yourself, shoot a basic sequence for protection before going all out artsy-craftsy. You'll be glad you did.

Learn to welcome criticism of your work. And learn to criticize yourself. It's the only way to progress. Every criticism, no matter how ridiculous it may seem, can tell you something about your work.

Don't bask in your successes—analyze them and find out why they worked, so you can repeat them. Use the same process to evaluate and learn from your failures. Professionalism is based on the ability to repeat your successes, and avoid repeating your failures.

Writing books, like making moving pictures, is also a subjective art. So I welcome your criticism of <u>my</u> work. If you have any ideas to improve future editions of THE BARE BONES CAMERA COURSE FOR FILM AND VIDEO, please contact me:

Tom Schroeppel   E-mail: Tom@TomSchroeppel.com
3205 Price Avenue   Website: www.TomSchroeppel.com
Tampa, FL 33611

INDEX

About the Author

Tom Schroeppel is a retired writer, director, cameraman, and editor living in Tampa, Florida. He worked in film and video for more than thirty years. His credits include documentaries, industrials and TV commercials throughout the United States and abroad. He also worked as a training consultant at television stations in Latin America and the Caribbean.

VIDEO GOALS:

Getting Results With Pictures And Sound

By
Tom Schroeppel

Also by Tom Schroeppel, author of
THE BARE BONES CAMERA COURSE FOR
FILM AND VIDEO,

**VIDEO GOALS: GETTING RESULTS
WITH PICTURES AND SOUND**

116 pages, 8 1/2 x 11

A practical guide to the entire
production process, from initial
concept to final edit.

"VIDEO GOALS is the kind of book everyone should read or reread
before a directing or editing session--it can help anyone do a
better and more professional job."

> Sandy Mielke
> Independent Producer/Director
> Miami, Florida

"Overall, a very valuable guide to the pragmatic elements of the
film and television production process. The text is clear,
honest and helpful, not pedantic."

> Jay B. Korinek
> Professor, Mass Communications
> Henry Ford Community College
> Dearborn, Michigan

PARTIAL CONTENTS: Planning the shape of your program, Establishing
a style, Writing dramatic and non-fiction scripts, Pre-production,
Directing the basic sequence, Directing to edit, Directing actors,
Selecting the appropriate microphone, Recording voices and
presence, Basic rules of editing, Editing sound, Selecting and
cutting music, Editing montages, Preparing for the sound mix, and
more.

TO: Tom Schroeppel
    3205 Price Avenue
    Tampa, FL 33611

Please send me _____ copies of *Video Goals: Getting Results With
Pictures and Sound* at $9.95 each, plus $3 postage/handling per book.

I enclose check or money order for _____ total.

Name (Please print)_____

Address_____

City _____ State _____ ZIP _____

Florida residents please add 6% state sales tax

Teachers: write on your letterhead for special volume discounts.

TO: Tom Schroeppel
    3205 Price Avenue
    Tampa, FL 33611

Please send me _____ copies of *The Bare Bones Camera Course for Film and Video* at $9.95 each, plus $3 postage/handling per book.

I enclose check or money order for _____ total.

Name (Please print)_____

Address_____

City _____ State _____ ZIP _____

Florida residents please add 6% state sales tax

TO: Tom Schroeppel
    3205 Price Avenue
    Tampa, FL 33611

Please send me _____ copies of *The Bare Bones Camera Course for Film and Video* at $9.95 each, plus $3 postage/handling per book.

I enclose check or money order for _____ total.

Name (Please print)_____

Address_____

City _____ State _____ ZIP _____

Florida residents please add 6% state sales tax

Teachers: contact me for special volume discounts.